DON'T BE THE EXIT

Escape the Retail Trap
- Outsmarting the Big Players -

ANIL P DEV

NOTION PRESS

NOTION PRESS

India. Singapore. Malaysia.

"This book is dedicated to my family and friends who have been a part of my journey in the markets."

Thank you!

Preface

"Retail is dead."

You've heard it before - maybe while scrolling headlines, maybe from a friend, maybe from a frustrated customer. Maybe, on your worst days, you've even said it yourself.

But here's the truth: retail isn't dead. What's dying is the **old way** of doing it. The version where loyalty was guaranteed, foot traffic was predictable, and your product alone was enough. That world doesn't exist anymore. And if you're not adapting, you're exiting - slowly, quietly, painfully.

I wrote this book because I've watched too many **individual retail traders** get squeezed out of a system that no longer makes room for them. Not because they weren't good at what they did. Not because they didn't hustle. But because no one told them the game had changed.

You're likely not a CEO, not a brand strategist, not a multi-store franchisee with a marketing department. You're the whole operation:

You do the buying.

You manage the stock.

You deal with customers - the good ones and the impossible ones.

You stay up late reconciling sales, figuring out what didn't sell and wondering what went wrong.

This book is for **you**.
It's a **warning** - and a **weapon**.

It's for the traders who set up every morning with hope and hustle, only to see the crowd thinning and the margins shrinking.

It's for the ones who feel invisible next to the giants, overwhelmed by online discounts and crushed by the convenience economy.

It's for those who've mastered their craft, but still feel like they're being slowly pushed out - one transaction at a time.

Why This Book? Why Now?

Because we're living in a world that doesn't favour the small trader anymore. The big players have speed, scale, and deep pockets. They're flooding the market with cheap goods, same-day shipping, and massive marketing budgets.

They don't just win on price - they win on data, psychology, and automation. And you're out there trying to compete with them while running your entire business from a counter, a stall, or a smartphone.

But here's the thing no one tells you:

You can outsmart them.

You can outlast them.

You can win - but only if you stop playing by their rules.

In **DON'T BE THE EXIT**, I'll show you how.

How to spot the early signs that your trade is under threat - before it's too late.

How to reposition yourself in a way that can't be easily copied, undercut, or replaced.

And how to shift your mindset from "barely getting by" to building something resilient, agile, and sustainable - even if you're operating on a shoestring.

This book is full of practical insights, field-tested strategies, and tough love. No fluff. No filler. Just the clarity you've been missing.

I've spent years observing what works - and what fails - for **individual traders** just like you. I've watched too many good people exit the game without ever being given the tools to stay in it.

This book gives you those tools.

Who This Book Is For - And Who It Isn't

If you're a single-person retail business - a trader working a market stall, a shop counter, a kiosk, or a small online storefront - this book is for you.

If you've ever stared at a quiet stall, wondered where the regulars went, or questioned whether the effort is still worth it - you'll find answers here.

If you're tired of being overlooked, undercut, and overwhelmed - you're not alone. This book is your blueprint for fighting back the smart way.

But let's be honest:

If you're looking for a quick fix, or expecting overnight success - this probably isn't for you.

This book is real. It's grounded. It asks you to work differently, think strategically, and stop waiting for things to "go back to normal."

This is not a motivational pep talk.

It's a survival manual - and a playbook for staying relevant when everyone else is giving up.

One Last Word Before You Start

I didn't write this book to tell you what you already know. I wrote it because I've seen people like you give up - not because they wanted to, but because no one ever showed them another way.

Inside these pages, you'll find a new perspective on the retail trap - and more importantly, how to escape it. You'll learn how to make smart moves, take bold steps, and hold your ground in a game that's always evolving.

This is not the end.

This is the beginning - of a new way to trade, a new way to win, and a new way to make sure *you* don't become the next quiet exit.

Let's begin.

Anil P Dev
Author of
DON'T BE THE EXIT

SECTION 1

THE INVISIBLE GAME – HOW RETAIL BECOMES EXIT LIQUIDITY

Chapter 1

The Exit Nobody Talks About

What is "Exit Liquidity"?

In every trade, someone is buying, and someone is selling. One side is entering with conviction. The other is exiting-with profit, relief, or regret. But in the grand chessboard of financial markets, especially during euphoric rallies or trend peaks, most retail participants don't realise one painful truth:

They are often the liquidity that allows someone else to exit.

Exit liquidity refers to the pool of eager market participants whose buying activity enables larger or more experienced players to offload their positions. It's not a term you'll find in glossy trading brochures or beginner guides. Yet, it's one of the most common and costly realities faced by the uninformed trader.

Retail traders typically enter when momentum is strong, news is positive, and sentiment is optimistic. Ironically, these are the exact moments when smart money looks to reduce exposure, lock in profits, and quietly walk out the back door.

What makes exit liquidity so deceptive is that it's **voluntarily provided**. Retail traders don't get forced into it-they offer it willingly, unknowingly. A large green candle, a strong earnings report, or a celebrity endorsement becomes the trigger. The retail trader thinks: "This is going higher." The professional thinks: "Perfect. You can buy what I need to sell."

The term "exit liquidity" might sound cold, but it's not a slur-it's a **function of market structure**. Every exit requires an entry. The question is: who's entering, and why? Most often, it's **those late to the move**, driven by emotion, not strategy.

What It Means to Be "Exit Liquidity"

To be exit liquidity means to enter the market just as someone else is leaving-usually after the price has already moved significantly. You're not catching the trend; you're absorbing its final breath.

It happens when:

You buy into a breakout that quickly fades.

You enter after a long rally, convinced the momentum will continue.

You buy at the top, believing you're getting in early-because the media, the influencers, and even the chart suggest so.

You're not alone. This is how the market works.

Retail traders often act on emotion-fear of missing out (FOMO), the excitement of crowd consensus, or the urgency of fast-moving prices. Institutions act on preparation. They anticipate these emotional reactions and structure their exits accordingly.

The most dangerous part of being exit liquidity is **the illusion of timing**. It *feels* like you've finally decided at the right moment. All indicators align. Social media agrees. The breakout is clean. But that's by design.

You're reacting to conditions that were **crafted to make you act**.

This is why the market punishes late conviction. Retail enters when risk appears low-but it's actually high because **everyone is positioned the same way**. Being exit liquidity doesn't mean you're always wrong-it means you're **the last to act** after the edge is gone.

How Institutions Build and Exit Positions

Institutions rarely buy aggressively into strength. They build positions during periods of low volatility, low interest, and low attention. This process is called **accumulation**-and it's slow, deliberate, and invisible to the average eye.

They use:

- Algorithmic order splitting to avoid detection.

- Volume absorption tactics to gather supply without triggering breakouts.

- News suppression to keep sentiment quiet until the position is built.

Then comes the exit.

Once their position is fully loaded, they begin to craft a narrative:

- Bullish analyst reports.

- Positive interviews with executives.

- Breakout patterns and technical confirmation.

As the story spreads and price moves higher, volume picks up. Retail joins in. The rally seems organic. But behind the scenes, smart money is selling-into strength, into optimism, into your conviction.

This methodical exit is often done through **liquidity windows**-breakouts above key levels, earnings announcements, or macro news spikes. Institutions **don't just take advantage of volatility-they manufacture it**.

They also scale out **strategically**, not emotionally. While a retail trader might hold for a round number or until "it feels right," professionals pre-plan exit zones:

- Just above previous resistance to capture momentum buyers,

- On peak volume days when demand is highest,

- During news-driven gaps where execution is instant.

Retail sees confirmation. Institutions see **completion**.

Lifecycle of a Trade: Smart Money Entry → Retail FOMO → Institutional Exit

Most trades follow a psychological curve. It starts with smart money entering quietly. Then price begins to rise. Retail begins to notice. Influencers start talking. Momentum builds. Volume increases. Everyone agrees: "This is going up."

At this point, smart money is already scaling out.

The retail trader, acting on emotion, not analysis, enters during the climax-often unaware that the very strength they're responding to is being sold into. When the reversal begins, it feels unjustified, sudden, and cruel. But it was predictable. It was a cycle.

This cycle often follows a 3-phase pattern:

1. **Accumulation** – Price stays range-bound. Volume is low. Nobody is watching.

2. **Markup** – Price breaks out. Sentiment shifts. Retail joins. News becomes favourable.

3. **Distribution** – Volume spikes. Momentum stalls. Smart money exits. Retail absorbs the risk.

The danger is that retail is conditioned to chase phase 2, **but they're entering into phase 3 without realising it**. They interpret rising volume as a sign of strength-when in reality, it's **a signal of exit.**

By the time the price falls, they blame news or manipulation. The truth?

They were part of a **well-scripted liquidity transfer.**

Why Most Retail Traders Are Always Late

Retail traders aren't foolish-they're just conditioned by the wrong cues. They rely on lagging indicators, crowd consensus, and media validation. They wait for confirmation, not context. They buy when it feels easy, not when it makes sense.

They enter:

- After the move.

- After the breakout.

- After the news.

But smart money entered before all of this. Not because they knew the future-but because they understood the cycle, the psychology, and the structure of how exits are engineered.

To stop being the exit, retail must shift:

- From reaction to preparation.

- From emotion to structure.

- From following noise to reading the script.

Being late is not just a timing issue-it's a **perspective issue**. Retail waits for clarity. Institutions trade into uncertainty because **they created the conditions for your clarity**.

Indicators confirm *after* the move.

Social sentiment peaks *after* the position has been built.

Retail gains confidence when it's **safest to exit, not enter**.

To stop being late, one must stop acting like a follower of price-and start thinking like a **creator of risk-reward asymmetry**.

Chapter 2

Retail vs Smart Money – A Game of Misdirection

The Illusion of Access: Low-Cost Trading, Influencer Culture, Gamification

At face value, it appears as though the playing field in financial markets has been levelled. Anyone with a smartphone and an internet connection can open a trading account, place a trade, and participate in the world's largest wealth-creation machine. Brokerage firms market freedom. Charting tools flash real-time data. Finfluencers post their daily profits, luring thousands with the message: "If I can do it, so can you."

But this sense of empowerment is manufactured, not earned. It is access without advantage-like giving a child a steering wheel in a Formula One car and calling it equality.

The brokers don't make money when you succeed. They make money when you trade-frequently, emotionally, and reactively. This is where gamification comes in:

- Celebratory animations when you complete your first trade.

- Leaderboards for "most active" users.

- Notifications that encourage you to "make your move now."

You are rewarded not for being profitable, but for being active.

Influencer culture adds another layer of misdirection. Trading becomes a performance. Screenshots of five-figure profits, jargon-filled trade recaps, and curated success stories dominate feeds. But rarely are the losses shown, the emotional breakdowns shared, or the risk taken acknowledged. Retail traders begin to chase not just profits-but identity validation through visibility.

This is how the illusion is maintained: You feel like a participant, but in reality, you're part of the script-a tool in someone else's exit strategy.

The mechanics behind this illusion go deeper. **Zero-commission brokers**, for instance, aren't offering free trades out of goodwill-they monetise you differently. Through a process known as **Payment for Order Flow (PFOF)**, they sell your orders to larger market makers, who execute them in a way that extracts micro-advantages for themselves. You're not just trading-you're *being traded against*.

Meanwhile, platforms leverage **behavioural science** to drive dopamine loops:

- Red-green colour schemes borrowed from casinos.

- Quick animations after trade execution.

- "You're on a streak!" prompts that psychologically nudge more trades.

It's not about helping you win.

It's about keeping you engaged long enough to extract value-from your habits, not your skill.

Accumulation vs Distribution: Where Smart Money Buys and Where It Sells

Smart money doesn't buy on green candles and Twitter tips. It accumulates in silence and distributes in noise.

Accumulation: Where the Crowd Sees Nothing

Smart money begins building positions during periods of invisibility-when price is consolidating in a range, volume is low, and sentiment is indifferent or even negative.

What appears to be a dull sideways movement is often the scene of deliberate accumulation. Institutions do not want their intentions to be noticed. They spread their orders across sessions and price levels, using volume absorption tactics to gather supply without causing breakout moves.

Clues of accumulation:

- Price holds support repeatedly, despite weak news flow.

- Volume appears on down days, but price doesn't collapse.

- Failed breakdowns occur, only to reverse upward quietly.

Retail traders typically avoid these phases. They perceive them as "dead money" zones. But these zones often precede significant trend emergence.

Distribution: Where the Crowd Sees Opportunity

Once the position is built and the narrative is ready, institutions begin the process of distribution-offloading their holdings to an increasingly enthusiastic crowd.

But unlike dumping, distribution is orchestrated. It occurs:

- Into rising volume and green candles.

- Amid bullish headlines, influencer endorsements, and positive momentum.

- While the public buys every dip, convinced the rally has just begun.

Clues of distribution:

- Price struggles to make new highs despite strong volume.

- Wicks appear at the top of candles, indicating selling into strength.

- News becomes euphoric, but price starts to stall.

The deception is elegant. Retail believes it is entering at the start. But it is unknowingly catching the baton from a party that is already leaving.

These cycles echo principles from **Wyckoff theory**, where the market is controlled by a 'Composite Operator'-a fictional representation of all smart money acting in coordinated fashion. The composite operator buys slowly, accumulates without noise, and only allows price to rise once the base is built.

During **accumulation**, large orders are hidden via **iceberg strategies**-only a portion of the total order is visible in the book. Algorithms detect weak hands and absorb volume at precise levels. All of this happens while retail watches the index or waits for the next headline.

During **distribution**, even bullish indicators play a role.

- RSI is strong? That's part of the exit mask.

- MACD confirms? That's when they sell to you. Even the chart structure often forms **ascending wedges**-stealth patterns of exit hidden beneath the illusion of strength.

By the time the breakout fails and price collapses, retail traders are left asking:

"What just happened?"

What happened was that you **entered into their exit plan**.

Social Proof, Sentiment, and the Exploitation of Herd Behaviour

Herd behaviour is not just a market phenomenon-it is a deeply human one. Psychologists have long studied our tendency to mimic others under uncertainty. In 1951, Solomon Asch's famous conformity experiment showed how individuals were willing to ignore objective reality just to agree with the majority.

The stock market is the modern equivalent of this experiment-repeated every day.

When people see others buying a stock, hyping it on forums, or talking about it on media, their brain interprets it as safety in numbers. It becomes easier to trust the crowd than to do individual thinking.

Institutions exploit this with surgical precision.

1. Creating the Crowd

They begin by:

- Sparking a breakout on low float stocks.

- Posting positive outlooks via media partners.

- Seeding discussions in social groups and influencer channels.

The price rises. The volume follows. The herd sees validation.

2. Steering Sentiment

Sentiment then becomes self-reinforcing. As more retail traders enter, their collective optimism amplifies the signal. Forums flood with predictions of new highs. YouTube thumbnails scream "100% potential". Traders stop questioning and start conforming.

Retail doesn't realise that what feels like consensus is often manufactured momentum.

3. Abandoning the Herd

Once the crowd is fully committed-long and confident-smart money withdraws liquidity. Price begins to stall, but sentiment lingers. Traders are too emotionally invested to see the signs.

Eventually, breakdowns occur. Panic replaces euphoria. The same social platforms that fuelled the rally now become echo chambers of fear.

This is not a coincidence. It's the rhythm of emotional misdirection.

A powerful behavioural flaw at play here is **social proof lag**-the tendency to act on what *has* worked for others, not what *is* likely to work for you. By the time a move trends on Reddit, Telegram, or YouTube:

- Smart money is either hedging,

- Or preparing to exit into the euphoria that's been manufactured.

These crowd-driven phases typically follow a **three-wave structure**:

1. Smart money initiates.

2. Media amplifies.

3. Retail floods in-too late.

This can be seen in meme stocks, altcoin pumps, and sector-specific hype waves. Retail joins at the peak of belief-when clarity is highest, and risk is greatest.

The Institutional Playbook: Engineered Emotion, Engineered Exits

Institutions do not operate on luck. They operate on control-over emotion, information, and execution. To exit a large position profitably, they need one thing above all: willing buyers.

And those buyers are created by engineered belief.

The institutional playbook is refined and adaptive. It includes:

- **Position Building**: During fear, silence, or indifference.

- **Narrative Seeding**: Spreading optimism through multiple channels at once.

- **Technical Triggers**: Using price structures to activate breakout buyers.

- **Volume Crafting**: Controlled bursts of activity to mimic momentum.

- **Media Leverage**: Timing interviews, upgrades, and opinion pieces to shape emotion.

Institutions don't predict crowds.

They build them.

They exit when the narrative peaks.

They distribute into the conviction that they helped create.

This is why trading alongside smart money requires more than chart reading. It requires seeing beyond the obvious, hearing what is not being said, and recognising that clarity often marks the top, not the beginning.

You must stop thinking like the crowd-and start seeing the scripts behind the movement.

Only then can you escape the trap of being the exit.

Many institutional strategies even align their exits with **index rebalancing events**, **earnings cycles**, or **sector rotation narratives**. They know precisely when the market's attention will shift-and use that shift to camouflage their intent.

Understanding this playbook means realising that you're not being traded with-you're being traded *around*.

Their edge is not just size or data.

It's **awareness of your reaction**, and the ability to pre-engineer your participation.

Chapter 3

The IPO Illusion – When Founders Exit, Retail Enters

High-Valuation IPOs and Post-IPO Crashes

On the surface, an Initial Public Offering (IPO) appears to be an exciting milestone-the debut of a company on the public stage, the first opportunity for retail investors to "get in early." But what is sold as an entry point for the masses is often an exit strategy for insiders.

High-valuation IPOs are often floated at peak hype, where the valuation far exceeds the company's fundamentals. The objective is not value creation but value extraction-to monetise years of private ownership by selling to a willing and emotionally charged public.

The pricing of these IPOs is carefully orchestrated. Investment banks underwrite and promote them, often through carefully crafted narratives, media endorsements, and selective financial disclosures. The valuation is justified using forward-looking projections, growth metrics taken out of context, and comparisons with unrelated high-growth peers.

Once listed, many of these stocks initially surge-fuelled by emotion, media coverage, and retail FOMO (Fear of Missing Out). But as reality sets in, earnings fail to match expectations, and insiders begin to offload more shares post-lock-in periods, the stock often crashes back to its true value-leaving retail investors trapped.

IPOs are not inherently bad. But when used as tools for insiders to exit at euphoric valuations, they become sophisticated liquidity traps-and the crowd, once again, becomes the exit.

What retail traders often miss is how the **demand curve is front-loaded before listing**. Investment banks conduct roadshows and encourage over-subscription, not to create fairness-but to build the perception of scarcity. The tighter the supply, the higher the demand appears-*even when the fundamentals are weak*.

Grey market premiums (GMPs) are floated ahead of the listing, amplifying the illusion of post-listing profits. But these premiums are often **speculative signals**, not backed by institutional conviction. Smart investors understand that the IPO pop is **not a guarantee**-it's a manufactured launchpad for early exits.

Retail investors, seduced by media buzz and oversubscription stats, end up buying into an **exhausted valuation**-not a new beginning.

How IPOs Serve as Liquidity Events for Insiders

Behind every high-profile IPO is a timeline the public never sees.

Founders, venture capitalists, and early-stage investors often hold equity purchased at a fraction of the IPO price. Their primary objective during an IPO is not to raise capital for growth-but to cash out.

These stakeholders typically go through the following phases:

- Seed and Series Funding Rounds: Ownership is acquired at steep discounts during private rounds.

- Valuation Build-up: Hype is created through rapid revenue growth, strategic partnerships, or simply narrative engineering.

- Pre-IPO Promotions: Publicity increases, financials are selectively showcased, and investment banks set the stage.

- IPO Day: The stock is listed, often at a steep valuation with tight supply to ensure early price spikes.

- Post-IPO Exit: After a mandatory lock-in period, insiders begin selling. Retail interest provides the liquidity.

Insiders are not necessarily acting maliciously. They are simply using the system to exit profitably. But retail traders, unaware of this internal motive, are drawn in by the surface story and become the perfect counterparty.

The IPO event is marketed as the company's coming-of-age moment. But for insiders, it's often a graduation party-a celebration of their ability to hand over risk at the highest possible valuation.

This exit strategy is often layered with **legal timing mechanisms**:

- Insiders agree to a **lock-in period** (typically 6–12 months), but as soon as it ends, large sell-offs quietly occur.

- These sales may be staggered to avoid panic-but if retail sentiment has faded, the stock drifts lower over time.

- Meanwhile, insiders may reduce further risk through **pre-IPO secondary placements** to institutional investors at a discount-*long before retail has a chance to participate*.

Many IPOs also include a clause allowing insiders to offload during stabilisation windows post-listing, especially if the price is supported by underwriters. These coordinated exits happen while media headlines still echo optimism.

The IPO is rarely a fundraising event for the business. More often, it's a fund transfer-from retail conviction to insider liquidity.

Analysing IPOs: Red Flags, Dilution, and Timing Traps

Retail investors are rarely equipped to evaluate IPOs with the same rigour as institutional players. As a result, they are prone to narrative traps and overlook critical warning signs.

Let's break down the most common red flags that signal a potential trap:

1. Excessive Valuation

If the IPO is priced aggressively relative to peers, with a Price-to-Earnings or Price-to-Sales ratio far above sector averages, caution is warranted. Often, the premium is justified by future projections rather than present fundamentals.

2. Large Insider Offer-for-Sale (OFS) Portion

When a significant percentage of the IPO consists of an offer for sale-meaning existing stakeholders are selling their shares rather than the company issuing new ones-it's a clue that the primary intent is exit, not expansion.

3. Recent Revenue Spikes or Profitability Surprises

Sudden growth spurts just before IPO filing should be scrutinised. Many companies inflate performance in the lead-up to an IPO through one-time deals, accounting manoeuvres, or unsustainable client wins.

4. Weak Post-Listing Float Management

If the IPO pop is followed by sustained weakness or insider selling after the lock-in expiry, it's a sign that support for the price was never organic-it was driven by engineered demand that has now evaporated.

5. Overpromised Narratives

Buzzwords like "disruptive," "tech-enabled," or "AI-powered" are often used liberally in IPO presentations. These terms draw attention but must be backed by evidence. When narrative outweighs substance, it often indicates valuation padding.

IPO investing requires a contrarian lens. Ask not just what is being sold, but why it is being sold now, and who is doing the selling. More often than not, the answer is: insiders are exiting-and retail is entering just as the music begins to fade.

To go deeper, retail investors should **study the DRHP (Draft Red Herring Prospectus)**-specifically:

- **Use of Proceeds**: Is the capital truly for growth, or just to clean the balance sheet?

- **Legal Risks**: Are there pending litigations or regulatory dependencies?

- **Peer Comparison**: Is the company cherry-picking metrics to appear better than it is?

Another trap is **IPO timing**. If the company has:

- No pressing capital needs,

- Is launching after a major index rally,

- Or is part of a "hot sector wave" (like electric vehicles or fintech)...

...then the IPO is likely a **liquidity capture**, not a business necessity.

Retail must also beware of the **IPO subscription hype**. Just because an issue is oversubscribed 10x does not mean it's safe. Institutions may only be applying for flip trades or short-term arbitrage.

Case Studies of IPOs Where Retail Became the Exit

Case Study 1: Paytm (India)

Once billed as the poster child of India's digital finance revolution, Paytm's IPO in 2021 was one of the largest in Indian history. It was priced at a valuation exceeding ₹1.4 lakh crore, despite the company being heavily loss-making.

- **What Went Wrong**:

The IPO had a large OFS component, indicating major stakeholders were exiting. The pricing was aggressive, and the business lacked a clear path to profitability.

- **Aftermath**:

The stock opened weak and fell over 27% on listing day, continuing its slide over the following months. Retail investors who bought into the IPO narrative were left holding steep losses, while early investors cashed out.

Case Study 2: WeWork (Global)

WeWork's IPO was famously pulled after its valuation collapsed from $47 billion to under $10 billion in a matter of weeks. The company's S-1 filing revealed governance issues, questionable financials, and overreliance on founder-led narrative.

- **What Could Have Been**:

Had the IPO gone through, insiders were positioned to exit at frothy valuations while the public bore the risk. In this case, regulatory scrutiny prevented a full-scale retail trap-but the intent was clear.

Case Study 3: Uber (Global)

Uber's 2019 IPO came with immense anticipation. Despite being a household name, the company had mounting losses, an unclear profitability path, and an inflated valuation based on growth potential.

- **What Happened**:

Uber listed at $45 per share but quickly fell below $30, burning early IPO investors. Insiders and private equity players began reducing their stake post-lock-in, locking in profits while the public faced price depreciation.

Case Study 4: Zomato (India)

Another hyped tech IPO in India, Zomato raised over ₹9,000 crore. Though initial listing was strong, the company faced a steep selloff later, particularly after pre-IPO investors like Info Edge started to trim their holdings.

- **Lesson**:

IPO euphoria fades quickly when institutional sellers use the rally as a liquidity window. Retail investors, caught in the afterglow, are left averaging down or exiting at losses.

Across these cases, one theme persists:

Narrative pulled them in, but structure locked them down.

In each IPO, early optimism was weaponised:

- Influencer commentary,

- High-profile media interviews,

- Selective financial storytelling.

Retail entered believing they were buying growth. What they were buying, however, was **the exit plan of someone who had entered long ago-and had already multiplied their capital quietly.**

Chapter 4

False Breakouts, Bull Traps & Hype Candles

How Technical Traps Are Created (Volume Spikes, Fake Breakouts)

The modern market landscape is flooded with retail traders leaning heavily on chart patterns, breakouts, and volume spikes as signals for opportunity. While technical analysis is a useful tool, it is far from immune to manipulation-especially when used in isolation.

A breakout is meant to signal strength-a confirmation that price has overcome resistance and may continue to move higher. But what if that breakout was never intended to hold? What if it was simply a trap engineered to lure buyers, create liquidity, and then reverse?

This is the anatomy of a false breakout-or more specifically, a bull trap.

Institutions understand that retail traders are watching certain chart levels: resistance zones, horizontal breakouts, and trendline breaches. When these levels are approached, liquidity builds-as buy-stop orders stack above resistance, waiting to be triggered.

Here's how the trap is set:

1. Price is slowly walked up to a known resistance level with controlled buying.

2. A sharp push is initiated above the level, triggering breakout traders and stop orders.

3. Volume spikes artificially as retail and algos join the move.

4. Institutions sell into this breakout liquidity-often completing their exit.

5. Price reverses sharply, trapping buyers in unfavourable positions.

Not all breakouts are traps-but many are too clean, too obvious, and too convenient. When a breakout feels "undeniable", and when everyone seems to agree, it may not be confirmation-it may be bait.

Institutions take this further by employing **multi-timeframe deception**. A breakout that looks solid on a 15-minute chart may be a mere wick or rejection on the 1-hour or daily chart. Retail, drawn to shorter timeframes, misses the broader structural context-and walks straight into the trap.

These moves are also reinforced by **technical confirmation bias**. Indicators like RSI, MACD, or even Super Trend might flash bullish at the very moment the trap is sprung. But these indicators are **reactive, not predictive**-they lag behind price and validate precisely when retail confidence peaks.

Moreover, institutions may use **iceberg orders**-hiding large sell positions behind small visible volumes-or time the breakout during **low liquidity hours** to maximise emotional reactions with minimal effort.

Euphoria Candles and Emotionally-Driven Entry Zones

Some candles don't represent opportunity-they represent emotion. And few emotions are as dangerous in the markets as euphoria.

A euphoria candle is a large, impulsive bullish candle-usually formed with strong volume and aggressive buying. It often follows a piece of news, an influencer recommendation, or a breakout above a well-known level. These candles ignite a feeling, not just a signal.

Retail traders interpret them as:

- Confirmation.

- Momentum.

- Institutional buying.

But in reality, many of these candles are the result of:

- Stop hunts: Triggering short stop-losses and creating artificial demand.

- Narrative timing: Positive news dropped precisely to coincide with distribution.

- Exhaustion moves: Final pushes before trend reversals.

The problem lies not in the candle itself-but in the psychology it creates:

- FOMO (Fear of Missing Out) sets in.

- Traders enter late, believing a trend is beginning.

- The price reverses swiftly-leaving late entrants trapped in loss.

These emotionally-driven entry zones are designed to overwhelm logic with urgency.

Retail buys not because of analysis-but because of how the candle makes them feel.

These are what we may call "signature spikes"-rapid, one-directional moves that offer no pullback, forcing traders to chase. These spikes often occur after:

- A sudden news announcement,

- A rumoured acquisition or regulatory nod,

- Or influencer-driven sentiment rallies.

Volume may appear to confirm the breakout-but a closer look often reveals that it's **imbalanced**. The volume is **front-loaded** and then dries up, revealing that the candle was more **exit than entry**.

Euphoria is dangerous not because of what it shows, but because of what it hides:

Institutional exit disguised as public enthusiasm.

Behavioural Finance and Pattern Manipulation

Markets don't just run on fundamentals or technicals. They run on behavioural responses-fear, greed, overconfidence, and panic.

Behavioural finance helps us understand that most market participants:

- Overreact to recent events.

- Anchor to past prices or patterns.

- Follow others rather than their plan.

Institutions know this. They don't need to manipulate traders directly-they manipulate the environment in which traders make decisions.

Examples of pattern manipulation:

- Fake breakouts: Triggering ascending triangle patterns, only to reverse.

- False support holds: Allowing price to bounce multiple times before snapping it on heavy volume.

- Head-fake candles: Long wicks above resistance that pull traders in before collapsing.

Retail traders are told to "trust the pattern." But smart money doesn't trust the pattern-they trust the reaction to it.

They use the predictability of retail behaviour around these patterns to design predictable traps.

The psychology is simple:

A pattern that's widely known becomes **a signal for institutions to exploit**, not follow.

One common tactic is **recycled failure**. A head-and-shoulders top fails, invalidating the bearish expectation, only to form a **larger head-and-shoulders** a few days later. By then, retail has given up or reversed their position-right before the true breakdown.

Repeated pattern failure also triggers **learned helplessness** in traders. After enough failed entries, they either stop trading the setup or abandon it just before it plays out-again offering perfect liquidity and psychological imbalance for smart money to capitalise on.

Patterns are visual tools.

But without **context, intent, and confluence**, they become **decorated illusions**.

Why Setups That "Look Too Good" Often Fail

One of the most painful lessons in trading is this:

The setups that feel safest are often the most dangerous.

Why?

Because when something "looks perfect"-it has likely already been seen by:

- Every retail trader.
- Every algo.
- Every market-maker.

And when too many people agree on a setup, it becomes a source of liquidity, not opportunity.

Smart money knows this. They understand that:

- The "picture perfect" cup-and-handle.
- The "textbook" flag breakout.
- The "ideal" Fibonacci bounce.

...are the places where the most retail volume will converge. That's not coincidence-it's strategy. The market needs liquidity to move, and nothing provides it better than a setup that looks too good to fail.

But here's the irony:

- If a setup is too good, it's usually too late.

- If everyone can see it, the move is likely done or about to reverse.

Real opportunity is often:

- Uncomfortable.

- Unclear.

- Contrarian in feel.

The professional doesn't wait for perfect-they wait for context. They trade:

- With confirmation, not consensus.

- With preparation, not persuasion.

If your entry is driven by how confident the chart looks-or how much Twitter agrees-you're not in a trade.
You're in a trap dressed as confidence.

This visual seduction of "perfect setups" is part of what we might call **trap aesthetics**. The chart is shaped in a way that appeals to trader psychology:

- Clean angles,

- Symmetry,

- Ideal ratios,

- Neatly drawn levels.

But perfect form often lacks **real substance**-there's no fresh demand behind the move, only **recycled liquidity from hope and confirmation bias**.

Institutions know that traders will front-run a pattern if it's too clean. So they let it build, **allow retail to enter**, and then:

- Dump into the breakout,

- Trigger stop-losses on the fake move,

- And re-enter at better value once liquidity is restored.

In markets, beauty often betrays.

The best trades are usually **a little ugly, a little uncomfortable, and a lot unnoticed.**

Conclusion and Key Takeaways

The Invisible Game – How Retail Becomes Exit Liquidity

What you've just uncovered is not a strategy-it is a revelation.

The market, at its core, is not merely a game of buying low and selling high. It is a **psychological arena**, where those who understand behaviour orchestrate the moves of those who only observe price.

Section 1 exposes a silent pattern that plays out daily on the charts-but is rarely spoken about in books, headlines, or online discussions. This is the **uncomfortable truth**: retail participants are not just late-they are often **used**.

Used to provide the **volume institutions need to exit**.
Used to absorb the risk that early players are offloading.
Used to **legitimise narratives** that insiders have already monetised.

From the life cycle of a trade (Chapter 1) to the engineered nature of emotion and exits (Chapter 2), to the IPO illusions and post-listing traps (Chapter 3), and finally to the hype candles and false breakouts designed to trigger emotion (Chapter 4)-you have now seen how **the illusion of opportunity becomes the mechanism of exploitation**.

But awareness is power.

The moment you see this game clearly, you are no longer just a player. You begin to operate as an observer-**strategic, selective, and emotionally detached.**

Key Takeaways

- **You are not invited to the party-you are the exit.** Most retail traders unknowingly enter markets at the precise moment smart money is leaving.

- **Liquidity is not found-it is created.** Institutions build exits through narratives, breakouts, and IPO hype. The more excited you are, the closer you likely are to the top.

- **What looks like opportunity is often engineered emotion.** Volume spikes, perfect patterns, and euphoric candles are designed not to inform, but to trigger participation.

- **Retail is never early-because retail waits for validation.** And by the time validation appears on the chart, **risk has already shifted**.

- **IPOs are not always opportunities-they are often structured exits.** When insiders sell and retail buys, the crowd doesn't get early access. They get priced in.

- **Every trap begins with belief.** When belief is shared, amplified, and celebrated-smart money prepares to exit. Because exits require one thing above all else: **believers.**

SECTION 2

INSIDE THE MIND OF SMART MONEY

Chapter 5: Strategic Exit Planning – How the Pros Unload

Engineering Liquidity Through Hype and Headlines

For large players in the market-institutions, funds, and insiders-exiting a position is not as simple as clicking 'sell'. When you're holding millions of dollars' worth of stock, you can't just dump it on the market without causing a sharp drop in price. So, the pros don't **sell into weakness**-they sell into **strength**, but strength they've often **engineered themselves**.

They understand that retail liquidity is not born-it is triggered. The most efficient way to create this liquidity is to control the story. And in today's markets, story spreads fast:

- Financial news channels.

- Analyst upgrades.

- Social media influencers.

- Earnings calls and media interviews.

Smart money uses these channels not to inform-but to inspire action. Action that generates buying interest. That buying interest then becomes the exit door they need.

What many traders don't realise is that these narratives are often **coordinated with technical setups**. For example, a bullish news article is timed just as price approaches a known resistance zone. The positive sentiment softens any fear and encourages breakout participation.

Simultaneously, institutions support price action with **controlled dips**, **order book manipulation**, and **strategic volume bursts** to make the move appear organic. In reality, it's often an ***engineered mirage***.

Furthermore, smart money often leverages **iceberg orders** (large orders broken into small visible chunks) and **algorithmic routing** to disguise exit intent. Retail sees a healthy uptrend; institutions are silently exiting into the illusion they've created.

The "Markup Stage" (Dow Theory Stage 2) and How Smart Money Exits Within It

Dow Theory defines market movement in stages-each one representing a different phase in the psychology of crowds and the action of professionals. Understanding these stages is essential for identifying where accumulation ends and exit begins.

Let's focus on Stage 2: The Markup Stage-where the trap is not a cliff, but a gentle incline that leads you right to the top, unknowingly.

During the markup stage, the market appears healthy. Breakouts confirm. Moving averages align. Sentiment flips bullish. Retail finally begins to believe.

But what they miss is that this is the very moment smart money is preparing to exit.

The pros never exit all at once. They scale out:

- Into rallies.

- Into breakout chasers.

- Into social media-fuelled demand.

Each rally during this stage is not just a price event-it is a liquidity window.

The smart money sells incrementally, ensuring price doesn't collapse and maintaining the illusion of strength just long enough.

In Wyckoffian terms, the **markup stage is the 'public participation phase'**. Institutions, having already accumulated in the base, now allow the crowd to validate the trend through momentum participation. This phase is often marked by:

- **Increased media coverage**, including endorsements from well-known investors.

- **Optimistic analyst reports**, often citing inflated price targets.

- **Sustained uptrend channels**, with shallow pullbacks that reinforce confidence.

However, if you observe closely, you may notice **distribution candles** beginning to appear-those with large upper wicks and rising volume but little progress. These subtle signals often mark the **beginning of institutional exit**, masked by the appearance of strength.

Time, Structure, and Psychological Pressure Points

Retail traders often focus only on price. But professionals pay attention to time and structure-because these are the two levers that can influence behaviour without touching the price.

Smart money understands the importance of timing exits when:

- Markets are euphoric.

- Volatility is low (reduces fear, enhances participation).

- Macro headlines are supportive.

They may hold through consolidation, waiting patiently for the moment when the emotional climate aligns with their exit objective.

This is not a random occurrence.

It is a calculated alignment of time and sentiment.

The pros don't think in terms of isolated price levels-they think in terms of zones, ranges, and behaviour. They look at:

- Where stops are likely clustered.

- Where retail traders will enter emotionally.

- Which structures (patterns or levels) will cause the most participation.

They then plan exits just beyond these levels. For example:

- A push above all-time highs.

- A spike beyond a symmetrical triangle.

- A run beyond a resistance that's been tested multiple times.

The trigger is never just price-it's the retail reaction to structure.

Smart money knows that retail participants tend to:

- Chase strength.

- Cut winners too early.

- Hold losers too long.

- Enter when they feel "safe".

The pro exit is planned precisely where retail traders feel safest.

Another critical element is **time-of-day and event-based timing**.

Exits are often planned:

- Just before or after **earnings releases**.

- During **FOMC meetings** or budget announcements.

- **Late in the trading session**, especially near the close when volatility compresses and order flow becomes more predictable.

Moreover, institutions understand **retail sentiment fatigue**. If a stock has rallied for several days, they wait for one final euphoric push-perhaps sparked by news or a sharp breakout-and then offload heavily into that spike. The sell-off is masked as a pullback... but the smart money has already exited, leaving retail holding the peak.

Selling Into Strength While Retail Buys the Peak

To sell effectively, someone else must be willing to buy. The best buyers?

Retail traders at the top.

Retail does not buy dips with confidence.

They buy confirmation-after a breakout, after news, after momentum.

They buy when it feels like a sure thing.

This emotional confidence is the exit trigger for professionals.

Institutions:

- Let the stock rally above a known high.
- Allow positive media to fuel sentiment.
- Watch as volume pours in from retail.
- Offload into this final wave of belief.

They sell into:

- Strength.
- Hope.
- Urgency.

Because they know that urgency equals liquidity.

Retail chases the move.

Institutions designed the move.

The tragic irony is this:

Retail sees the rally as the beginning.

But it is actually the end.

The move was not about breakout-it was about exit.

This concept is especially prevalent in **high-beta stocks and small-caps**, where even a moderate institutional exit can spark steep reversals. Smart money uses ***false breakouts*** (or "bull traps") to pull in demand:

- A stock breaks out on strong volume.

- Sentiment peaks on social media.

- Chartists declare a fresh leg up.

Yet within two sessions, price fails to follow through.

Why?
Because the breakout wasn't a signal-it was an engineered exit point, designed to attract late money.

Retail traders see confirmation.

Institutions see liquidity.

If you find yourself entering when price "finally breaks out," ask yourself:

Who is selling to me-and why now?

Chapter 6

The Mechanics of a Setup vs a Setup for the Crowd

The Difference Between True Technical Confluence and Coincidental Signals

To the untrained eye, a setup is a setup. If multiple indicators align-be it RSI, MACD, moving averages, or price action-the average retail trader assumes confirmation. But the reality is more nuanced.

True technical confluence is when multiple signals, derived from different methodologies or timeframes, align within a broader context that supports the trade idea. It reflects structural integrity, alignment of momentum, trend, and volume.

Coincidental signals, on the other hand, occur when indicators appear to align purely due to lag or mathematical overlap. These setups often look compelling but lack depth, strength, or institutional backing.

Retail traders, drawn to visual alignment and simplicity, often fail to distinguish between the two. As a result, they enter based on apparent confluence, unaware that the structure lacks institutional intent.

True confluence is often quiet-it doesn't scream from the chart. It's found when:

A major moving average coincides with a **price structure zone** (not just any line).

Volume supports the breakout *before* price confirms.

A higher timeframe bias is respected by lower timeframe triggers.

Coincidental confluence is deceptive. For example:

- RSI is oversold, MACD crosses bullish, and price touches a fib level-**but it's all against the prevailing trend**.

- Multiple indicators "align" on the same timeframe, but there is **no participation from broader structure or sentiment**.

- A breakout candle is large-but follows a prolonged rally with **diminishing volume** and poor context.

Retail mistakes alignment for confluence. Smart money looks for **structure, intention, and imbalance**-not just checkmarks on a chart.

How Institutional Players Create a Setup to Trap Retail

Institutions do not wait for signals-they create them. The setups you see on charts are not always organic. In many cases, they are engineered-designed to lure participation, trigger algorithms, and generate liquidity.

A setup for the crowd typically involves:

- A well-known pattern (triangle, flag, double bottom).

- Positive momentum confirmed by volume and indicators.

- News or sentiment supporting the move.

Once this alignment is visible to retail traders, smart money positions on the other side.

They may:

- Push price slightly above resistance to activate breakout buys and stop-losses.

- Absorb that volume without letting price advance further.

- Reverse the move rapidly, trapping participants and collecting liquidity.

This is not always manipulation. It's simply exploitation of predictability.

Retail setups are not just visible-they're telegraphed:

- Trendlines drawn by millions of traders become **self-fulfilling magnets**.

- Breakout levels are publicly discussed on forums, YouTube, or Twitter.

- Everyone sees the same pattern-and acts the same way.

Institutions use this visibility as a weapon. They initiate:

- A **stop-run** just above the obvious level,

- Create a sharp wick to trap breakout buyers,

- Let price linger briefly to give retail a false sense of security,

- Then unwind the move-slowly or violently.

The true setup for smart money includes:

- A backdrop of **accumulation or distribution,**

- A clearly identified **imbalance in positioning,**

- Liquidity pools on the other side of the structure.

It's not the setup that matters-it's **who controls the trap and who supplies the trigger.**

Examples of Failed Breakouts and Their Behavioural Underpinnings

Failed breakouts are not just technical events-they are behavioural ones. They often reflect the moment when crowd belief reaches its peak-and smart money seizes the opportunity to reverse the narrative.

Example 1:

A stock breaks above multi-month resistance with a large bullish candle and surging volume. Social media explodes with bullish calls. Retail rushes in. Two candles later, the stock reverses hard, trapping breakout buyers.

What happened?

- The breakout was too clean, too popular.

- Volume spiked-but it was one-sided.

- Institutions used the breakout as an exit.

Example 2:

A cryptocurrency shows a textbook inverse head and shoulders. Breakout occurs. Price rises slightly, stalls, then collapses.

What happened?

- The pattern was widely shared online.

- The breakout level attracted retail volume.

- Smart money absorbed liquidity and reversed the trend.

These aren't just failed patterns-they are **crowd-triggered liquidity events**. They show that setups don't fail on their own. They fail because **belief becomes consensus, and consensus becomes risk**.

Let's break down what's really happening behind these examples:

- In **Example 1**, the volume spike wasn't organic. It was a **reaction to engineered price movement**-meant to create emotional urgency. Retail bought strength. Institutions sold into that strength.

- In **Example 2**, the inverse head and shoulders was **front-run by smart money**, who began building short positions before the right shoulder completed. By the time the breakout occurred, they were ready to reverse price *into trapped buyers*.

These failed breakouts teach one vital truth:

The market rewards **early preparation**, not emotional reaction.

Retail rarely asks: "Why is this setup occurring now?" They only ask: "Is it confirmed?"

And that's how confirmation becomes a coffin for capital.

Pattern Reliability vs Manipulated Context

Patterns work. Until they don't.

Retail traders often treat patterns as certainties. They back-test flag formations, inverse head and shoulders, double bottoms-and conclude statistical reliability. But what those tests don't account for is context-especially in modern, manipulated markets.

Patterns without context are illusions.

A bull flag in a strong uptrend with rising volume, supportive sentiment, and sector strength has weight. The same pattern after a parabolic run, with weakening volume, overstretched RSI, and crowd hype-becomes bait.

Institutions know this. They allow patterns to form. Sometimes, they help shape them. And when the structure is loaded with retail belief, they strike.

The pattern didn't fail. The context did.

Context is more than trend-it includes:

- **Where** the pattern forms (after accumulation or at exhaustion?),

- **How** volume behaves (is participation increasing, or are insiders exiting?),

- **What** sentiment surrounds it (is it ignored or glorified?).

A breakout from a bull flag in an obscure mid-cap, trading quietly for weeks, may offer true opportunity.

But the same flag-widely circulated on finfluencer feeds, showing confluence on three oscillators, and aligned with an earnings headline-becomes **a setup for the crowd**, not for profit.

Smart money trades **around patterns**, not because of them.
They trade the **emotional reaction to the pattern**, not the structure itself.

To rely on patterns without reading their context is like reading sheet music and expecting a symphony to play itself.

Chapter 7: News, Narratives, and Noise

News as a Distribution Tool

In theory, news is meant to inform. In practice, it is often used to influence. Institutions understand the power of timing. Good news is rarely shared at random. It's coordinated, managed, and strategically released when the crowd needs encouragement-or distraction.

Retail traders tend to chase headlines. A bullish announcement? Buy. A glowing article? Enter. A well-timed acquisition press release? Load up. But what if the news wasn't meant for you to act on-but for someone else to exit?

This is the reality behind many news-driven rallies. Institutions don't react to the news-they use it. Once their positions are built, they need volume-urgency, belief, and liquidity. News becomes the spark. Retail becomes the fuel. Distribution happens not after news, but *during* the euphoria it creates.

News works best as a distribution tool when it's **anticipated, controlled, and layered with technical triggers**. Institutions often ensure that news:

- Drops near resistance or breakout zones,

- Coincides with momentum indicators flashing green,

- Aligns with favourable market mood or macro events.

These layered signals give the illusion of confirmation. But what's really happening is **sentiment engineering**.

The smarter institutional desks may even **front-load** the rally-buying quietly before the news, then allowing the headline to create demand for their exit. By the time retail traders are reacting to the story, **the move has served its purpose**.

Price doesn't rise because of news.

It rises so **the news can be sold into**.

Earnings Hype, Upgrades, Management Appearances

Earnings seasons are among the most emotionally charged times in the market. Analysts issue upgrades. CEOs appear on business channels. "Beating expectations" becomes the buzz phrase.

But beneath the numbers, something else is happening.

Earnings are rarely about the raw data-they're about expectations. A company may report strong revenue, but if the stock has already rallied hard, it may still sell off. Why? Because the news was already priced in-and the crowd had already bought.

This is when institutions exit. They allow price to rise into earnings. They create excitement with upgraded targets. Management appears confident, smiling on screen. And just when retail is convinced the stock is going higher, selling begins.

The distribution is masked by optimism. But the smart money is already gone.

Earnings hype is not accidental-it's **a strategic moment to influence sentiment** while executing exits. Consider the cues:

- **Pre-earnings rallies** are not always organic-they're often *positioning moves*.

- **Management language** becomes unusually positive-emphasising future growth, not present results.

- **Broker upgrades** may come after a price run-up-further luring retail in.

Once the earnings call is over, institutional desks watch **one thing: *reaction***. If the reaction is euphoric, they sell into the surge. If the stock gaps up, they distribute during the first hour spike. If guidance is strong but momentum stalls, it's a cue that the buying is exhausted.

Retail interprets this post-earnings weakness as "profit booking" or "confusion."

But it's often just **planned exit timing**.

Understanding When "Good News" is Priced In

One of the most common traps for retail investors is assuming that good news will drive a stock higher-regardless of timing, context, or prior price movement.

But the market is a forward-looking mechanism. It doesn't reward news-it rewards surprise.

If a company reports a strong quarter, but the stock has already rallied for weeks, there may be little room left for upside. Institutions that bought during consolidation now sell into the strength. Retail, late to the party, buys the headline-and holds the top.

This is when "good news" doesn't lead to good returns. Because the edge was in being early-not in reacting late.

A useful question for any trader to ask is:

"Who doesn't know this already?"

If the answer is "no one," the news is priced in. Smart money prices in expectations **well in advance** of public headlines. They assess sentiment, market positioning, and valuation *before* the news breaks.

Common signs that good news is already priced in:

- The stock **doesn't rally** on the news-it consolidates or dips.

- The move **feels stale**-volume surges, but price doesn't follow.

- The **crowd already anticipated it**-forums and media were bullish days earlier.

Understanding this concept is critical because reacting to good news **without considering context** is how retail becomes **liquidity, not strategy**.

Media Psychology and Its Impact on Price

The media doesn't predict price-it reflects emotion.

By the time a stock hits the headlines, it's usually because price has already moved. When it shows up on prime-time shows or front-page finance articles, the crowd is already watching-and likely already participating.

Media narratives follow price. They don't lead it.

Smart money knows this. They understand that the louder the media gets, the closer the move is to completion. So they use this visibility to exit. While the public watches interviews and reads bullish headlines, the pros unwind their positions-quietly, strategically, and without resistance.

Retail buys because the media says so. Institutions sell because the media *finally* said so.

Media psychology thrives on **storytelling, not analysis**. It frames stocks as underdogs, winners, disruptors, or comeback stories. These narratives are emotionally potent-but they have little to do with real timing.

When media coverage spikes:

- Retail sees opportunity.
- Institutions see **attention**-which equals liquidity.

Price and media often share this sequence:

1. Institutions accumulate quietly →
2. Price rises →
3. Media notices →
4. Crowd joins →
5. Institutions exit →

6. Price stalls or reverses.

It's not that the media lies.

It's that they arrive **just in time for the exit.**

Conclusion and Key Takeaways

Inside the Mind of Smart Money

You have now stepped beyond the surface and into the **engine room of the market**-where decisions are not made in reaction to candles, but in orchestration of crowd behaviour. Section 1 revealed how the retail trader is used. Section 2 has shown you **how that use is planned**.

The core insight?

Smart money doesn't trade against price-they trade **against people**.

Against impatience. Against crowd confirmation. Against retail emotion.

Where retail sees patterns, smart money sees **trap potential**.
Where retail sees news, institutions see **liquidity events**.
Where retail sees momentum, smart money sees **exit ramps**.

From understanding how liquidity is engineered through headlines and hype (Chapter 5), to how setups are framed for the crowd but used for exits (Chapter 6), and how media, earnings, and sentiment create noise that masks smart money behaviour (Chapter 7)-this section teaches you that **every visible move has an invisible motive**.

This is not paranoia. It is preparation.

Because once you learn to read market behaviour as **intent**, not just motion, you start to participate **strategically**, not emotionally.

Key Takeaways

- **Smart money doesn't chase price-they build exits.** They accumulate quietly and distribute loudly-into your belief, not their own.

- **The markup stage is not where institutions buy-it's where they leave.** Retail often enters late, thinking they've spotted a trend. Smart money uses this moment to offload.

- **True setups are contextual, not visual.** What looks like a breakout may be a trap. What looks like confirmation may be manipulation. Without context, patterns are illusions.

- **News is not information-it's distribution.** Headlines are timed to match market positioning. The moment it feels like everyone knows, **someone is quietly selling.**

- **Media doesn't predict price-it reflects emotion.** When the story finally becomes popular, the smart money story is already over.

- **Institutional strategy is not complex-it's controlled.** They do not outsmart retail by intelligence. They outwait, outthink, and outsell the crowd.

This section was your entry into **the other side of the market mirror.** You've seen how institutions think, how they plan exits, how they use price, time, sentiment, and psychology to create opportunities-**not for you to enter, but for them to leave**.

In the final section, we shift from understanding the game to mastering your place in it. No longer the liquidity. No longer the follower. The next step is to trade smarter-**not just with knowledge, but with clarity, conviction, and control**.

SECTION 3

DON'T BE THE EXIT – HOW TO TRADE SMARTER

Chapter 8

Reversing the Role – From Exit Liquidity to Informed Trader

Identifying Signs of Distribution (Volume Anomalies, Failed Rallies)

The difference between a healthy uptrend and a distribution phase lies not in the price alone-but in **how** price moves, and **who** is participating.

Distribution is when smart money exits. But unlike panic-driven sell-offs, distribution happens **quietly**. Price may even continue rising during this phase-but the engine behind the move has already shifted.

Key signs include:

- **Volume anomalies**: Unusually high volume on sideways or weak price action.

- **Failed rallies**: Price spikes that reverse quickly, often with long upper wicks.

- **Bearish divergence**: Indicators flatten or decline while price pushes higher.

These are not obvious signs. That's the point. Distribution is designed to look like strength-until it's over.

To identify distribution effectively, traders must learn to **watch behaviour, not just bars**. For example:

- If price rises sharply but volume declines, it could signal **a lack of real demand**.

- If volume increases on **down days**, but price recovers slowly after, it may mean **insiders are quietly exiting into strength.**

Another giveaway is the **"churn effect"**-where price stays within a range despite strong news or apparent momentum. This is a classic sign that large players are **absorbing buying pressure**, not adding to it.

Moreover, failed breakouts near highs-especially after a sustained run-signal exhaustion. When these rallies reverse swiftly, trapping breakout buyers, it's not weakness by accident. It's **smart money using strength to hand off risk.**

To stay informed, stop asking, *"Is price going up?"* Start asking, *"Who is still buying-and who is already done?"*

Recognising Sentiment Extremes and Retail Exhaustion

Market tops don't form when people are fearful. They form when **everyone believes the move is obvious, inevitable, and risk-free.**

Sentiment extremes occur when retail conviction is at its highest. You'll hear phrases like:

- "This stock can't go down."

- "The dip will be bought."

- "Everyone is bullish. It's just the beginning."

Retail exhaustion, ironically, comes **not from fear, but from confidence**. When everyone is already in, there's no one left to buy. That's when price begins to stall-and eventually reverses.

One of the most overlooked indicators of a potential top is **unanimity**. When analysts, influencers, and financial media are all singing the same bullish tune, it's no longer insight-it's **echo chamber sentiment**.

Examples of sentiment extremes include:

- Parabolic price action accompanied by retail euphoria on social media.

- Stocks trending on financial television and chat rooms simultaneously.

- FOMO-driven entries becoming a dominant reason to participate.

Retail exhaustion often follows this euphoria. It's visible through:

- Shrinking candles on strong volume (people are buying, but price isn't progressing).

- Heavy positioning in call options with declining open interest.

- Emotional fatigue in forums-where doubt creeps in, yet hope keeps traders holding.

The key shift is this:

When people stop asking *if* to buy and start asking *how much*, the crowd is no longer analysing-they're surrendering to momentum. That's when smart money starts to **reverse their stance silently**.

Reading Price Action with Context, Not Emotion

Price action is more than candlestick patterns-it's the **language of intent**.

Retail traders often read candles emotionally. A green bar means bullishness. A red bar means weakness. But price action means nothing **without context**.

Context includes:

- The **location** of the move (support, resistance, supply zones).

- The **volume** behind the move (is it supported, or thin and reactive?).

- The **sequence** of moves before and after (is this continuation or distribution?).

A strong bullish candle after a breakdown could be a **dead cat bounce**. A bearish engulfing candle at resistance could be **institutional unloading**. Without context, all patterns are misleading.

Context requires a shift in perception. For instance:

- A bullish candle at the **top of a range** after a long uptrend isn't strength-it could be a **trap**.

- A red candle on **low volume** at support might not mean panic-it could be a **liquidity sweep** before reversal.

Consider the idea of **trap candles**:

- Large green bars that **pierce resistance**, followed by tight consolidation or reversal.

- Bearish engulfing patterns that occur **just below breakout zones,** luring in short sellers before the squeeze.

Understanding context also means studying **what price is** *not* **doing**:

- Is it reacting strongly to news-or is it ignoring it?

- Is it following the market index-or diverging from it?

When price **hesitates at key zones**-especially with increasing volume-it signals a battle. If retail sees it as confirmation, but smart money sees it as opportunity to offload, the outcome becomes predictable.

Your job as an informed trader isn't to react to the candle.
It's to **understand why the candle appeared where it did-and what preceded it.**

How to Anticipate Smart Money Movement

Anticipation is not prediction. It is preparation.

Smart traders don't try to guess tops or bottoms. They look for signs-subtle shifts in structure, volume, and behaviour-that suggest accumulation or distribution.

Key habits that help anticipate smart money:

- Study **volume and range**-wide candles with heavy volume often indicate intent.

- Observe **retests**-a second touch of a level with muted volume suggests fading interest.

- Watch **liquidity zones**-price often reacts violently at prior supply or demand zones.

More than anything, learn to recognise **silence before movement**. Smart money enters before the crowd-during boredom, not excitement.

Anticipation also means learning the **tempo** of smart money:

- They accumulate when price is boring-**during long consolidations** where volatility compresses.

- They distribute as price climbs in a controlled, stair-step fashion-**never in panic**.

Look for:

- **Volume asymmetry**: Where up moves have controlled volume, but down moves spike erratically (a sign of stealthy exits).

- **Stop runs followed by rejections**: Classic institutional tactics to clear liquidity pools before real moves.

- **Divergence between sectors or indices**: Smart money rotates-not all strength is real, and not all weakness is accidental.

One subtle tell: **non-participation in a breakout**. When a stock breaks out of a range but **fails to gain momentum**, despite news and volume, it often signals a **dry-up in institutional support**.

The informed trader doesn't follow smart money step by step.
They recognise the **environment smart money prefers**, the **tools they use**, and the **conditions under which they act**.

Your edge is not in seeing what they do-
It's in preparing for where they are **most likely to act
next.**

Chapter 9

Contrarian Thinking with Confirmation

"Don't Fight the Trend" vs "Don't Follow Blindly"

One of the oldest pieces of trading wisdom is: "Don't fight the trend." And in principle, it's sound advice. Trying to short a strong uptrend or buy a falling knife without context is a fast path to loss.

But the problem is not the trend-it's the **blind obedience to it**.

Following a trend without understanding the structure, context, or sentiment driving it is no better than fighting one. Many retail traders confuse trend-following with safety, assuming that as long as price is going up, it must continue.

Smart traders don't just follow trends-they qualify them.

They ask:

- Is this trend fuelled by genuine accumulation or crowd emotion?

- Has the trend extended beyond reasonable reward-to-risk?

- Are institutions participating-or exiting?

The goal is not to oppose the trend, but to think critically about it. Sometimes, the smartest move is to pause, not pursue.

A healthy trend is not just about higher highs or lower lows. It's about who is participating and how price is behaving around key levels. The market may still be trending, but if:

- **Volume is drying up** on rallies,

- **Momentum is weakening**, or

- **Sentiment is euphoric**...

...it may no longer be a trend worth following-it may be a **trap waiting to spring**.

True contrarian thinking isn't about being early. It's about **seeing when the crowd stops thinking**. A contrarian is not someone who trades against price-they trade against **complacency**. And complacency is most dangerous at trend extremes.

Confirmation Tools: Sentiment, Structure, and Smart Money Footprints

Contrarian thinking doesn't mean acting without evidence. It means waiting for **confirmation from the right signals**-not from popularity or excitement.

Three tools can help validate whether a contrarian idea holds weight:

a) Sentiment

Look for extremes in optimism or fear.

- Is the crowd too confident?

- Is everyone aligned on one side of the trade?

- Are analysts and influencers unusually quiet or loud?

Sentiment helps you measure the emotional imbalance behind price.

b) Structure

Is price at a key zone?

- Has it returned to a previous breakout point?

- Is it forming a higher low, or breaking structure?

Structure provides the **technical backdrop** for timing and risk management.

c) Smart Money Footprints

Use volume, positioning, and behaviour to infer smart money intent.

- Are large volumes appearing without price progress?

- Is there absorption at supply or demand zones?

Smart money doesn't leave a note-but they leave a trail.

These tools are most powerful when used **together**.

For example:

- A major resistance zone is tested.

- Sentiment is highly bullish.

- Volume spikes, but price fails to move higher.

- And you notice large sell wicks or failed breakouts.

This is not just structure. It's not just sentiment. It's a convergence of **warning signs**-and that's when a contrarian idea moves from theory to action.

Smart traders don't guess-they wait for alignment between **emotion, behaviour, and price geometry**.

Look not for what you want to see, but for what's being **telegraphed by the tape**-especially when it contradicts what the crowd believes.

The Concept of "Late and Right" over "Early and Wrong"

Retail traders often feel pressure to "get in early." They fear missing the move. They rush into trades, hoping to catch the bottom or top before others do. But in doing so, they frequently enter too soon, without confirmation.

Smart traders embrace the idea of being "late and right" instead of "early and wrong."

Entering slightly later-but with clarity, structure, and confirmation-offers:

- Better risk-to-reward ratios.

- Higher probability setups.

- A more stable mindset.

You don't need to catch the bottom. You just need to catch the middle-with conviction.

Being early might feel like bravery. But in trading, **precision is not about timing the first tick-it's about catching the** *right* **moment within the cycle**.

Entering late but with proper context means:

- You're riding with momentum, not against it.

- You're seeing evidence of smart money participation.

- You're trading into clarity-not chaos.

Retail traders often view delayed entries as "missed opportunities." But professionals see it as **waiting for validation**-allowing the market to prove its intent.

Missing the first 5% of a move is irrelevant if the next 20% is clean, controlled, and contextual. Missing a move entirely is better than forcing a position in search of ego gratification.

Late and right beats early and exposed-**every time**.

Patience as a Trading Edge – The Sniper Mindset

Impatience is one of retail's greatest liabilities. The need to always be in a trade, to always be doing something, leads to overtrading, emotional decision-making, and poor entries.

Smart money doesn't trade all day. They wait. They study. They strike only when conditions are optimal.

This is the **sniper mindset**-a patient, deliberate, and disciplined approach to execution.

It involves:

- Defining clear trade criteria.

- Waiting for confluence and confirmation.

- Ignoring distractions, rumours, and noise.

The sniper doesn't chase. He observes. He knows the value of one well-placed shot over a hundred random bullets.

The same is true for the informed trader.

The sniper mindset requires **preparation before participation**. Every great trade is earned **before the trigger is pulled**-through observation, analysis, and clarity.

In practice, this means:

- Marking levels before the session.

- Knowing what confluence must occur before entry.

- Having the discipline to **walk away when conditions aren't ideal**.

Patience protects capital.

Patience protects confidence.

Patience protects clarity.

Most traders lose not because their strategy is flawed-but because their **timing is impatient and their entries are unfiltered**.

The sniper knows this. He doesn't just wait-he waits **with intent**. And that's the edge retail often ignores in their quest to always be in the action.

Chapter 10

Mastering the Psychological Game

The Emotional Warfare: Fear, Greed, Hope, FOMO

The market is not a place of logic. It's a battlefield of emotion-where fear and greed shape decisions more than facts and figures.

Retail traders lose not because they lack strategy, but because they lack control over:

- **Fear** of losing money.

- **Greed** to make more than necessary.

- **Hope** that a bad trade will turn around.

- **FOMO**-the fear of missing out when others seem to be winning.

These emotions distort perception, cloud judgement, and trigger irrational behaviour.

They make traders:

- Exit too early on winners.

- Hold onto losers far too long.

- Chase price without confirmation.

The most dangerous time in the market is not when things are unclear. It's when emotion overrides structure.

Emotions aren't just reactions-they're predictable vulnerabilities.

Smart money understands that the crowd behaves in patterns:

- Fear spikes near bottoms, creating **panic-driven exits**.

- Greed intensifies after breakouts, creating **perfect exit liquidity**.

- Hope paralyses traders from cutting losses.

- FOMO creates impulsive entries with no plan.

This emotional sequence happens again and again:

1. Missed opportunity →

2. FOMO entry →

3. Initial gain →

4. Drawdown →

5. Hopeful holding →

6. Panic sell →

7. Regret →

8. Re-entry at the wrong time.

Understanding the cycle is not enough. To stop being the exit, one must **actively disrupt it**.

How Smart Money Trades Against Human Nature

Smart money doesn't just trade price-they trade **the crowd's psychology.**

They study how retail behaves under pressure, and they build their strategies accordingly. If the average trader panics during volatility, institutions inject it. If retail gets euphoric after strong moves, they create those moves.

Smart money:

- **Accumulates during boredom.**

- **Distributes during excitement.**

- **Manipulates patterns** that trigger crowd responses.

- **Waits** while others rush.

They trade not against individuals-but against the **predictability of human emotion.**

Markets aren't random. They are arenas of **collective behaviour.** And because human nature is stubbornly consistent, it's also consistently exploited.

Smart money doesn't need to manipulate every tick-they just need to:

- Recognise where the crowd will react,

- Anticipate the emotion that reaction will trigger,

- And position themselves **one step ahead.**

For example:

- They allow a bullish flag to form... and then **trigger FOMO** just before fading the move.

- They sell into spikes because they know **greed creates urgency**, and urgency creates volume.

- They wait for exhaustion, not because they're patient-but because they know **patience pays when others are desperate**.

Retail trades based on emotion.

Smart money trades **against it**-because they trust the crowd to always repeat the same mistakes.

Tools for Discipline: Journaling, Reflection, Reset Routines

Mastering the psychological game requires more than awareness-it demands practice. And the best way to build emotional discipline is to develop systems that anchor your behaviour.

a) Journaling

Writing down your trades, reasoning, emotions, and outcomes provides:

- Clarity on patterns and repeated mistakes.

- A mirror to your impulsive decisions.

- Evidence of progress or delusion.

b) Reflection

After each session or week, reflect on:

- What you did well.

- What you ignored.

- What you felt-but didn't act on.

Reflection turns experience into insight.

c) Reset Routines

A losing streak isn't just financial-it's mental. Develop routines to reset:

- Step away from screens.

- Meditate, walk, or journal.

- Revisit your trading plan-not the market.

Discipline isn't found in willpower alone. It's built through structure.

The greatest traders aren't emotionless-they're **self-aware.**

Journaling should go beyond price:

- What did I feel before I clicked 'buy'?

- Was this trade part of the plan, or a reaction?

- Did I size the position emotionally or strategically?

Reflection is not about blame-it's about **observation without judgement**.

You cannot fix what you refuse to see.

Reset routines are your circuit breakers:

- After a drawdown, step back before revenge trading.

- After a big win, avoid overconfidence-fuelled overtrading.

- After five trades in a row-pause and assess clarity, not just P&L.

Discipline is not rigidity.

It's the art of returning to your centre, no matter what the market throws at you.

Why Mental Clarity Is More Important Than Indicators

In the modern trading world, information is everywhere. Tools, indicators, signals, algorithms. But despite all this technology, most traders still struggle.

Why? Because they lack **mental clarity**.

Indicators are useless if your judgement is clouded. Strategies don't work if your state of mind is impulsive.
No amount of data can substitute for a clear mind.

Mental clarity allows you to:

- Stick to your process.

- Avoid revenge trades.

- Respect risk when it matters most.

It is your ultimate filter-the one thing that ensures **you don't become the exit.**

Clarity precedes execution. When your mind is clean:

- You don't seek confirmation-you look for structure.

- You don't chase-you wait.

- You don't hope-you plan.

Clarity also means knowing when **not to trade**:

- When you're tired, emotional, or unsettled.

- When markets are choppy or context is missing.

- When your desire for action outweighs the opportunity.

Many traders blame indicators. But it's not the tool- it's the hand that wields it.

Mental clarity is what allows you to:

- Say *no* to average setups.

- Respect your stop-loss instead of rationalising it.

- Exit without fear, and re-enter without revenge.

Smart money isn't smarter because of better indicators.

They're smarter because their **decision-making is calm, disciplined, and deliberate**.

That clarity-more than any strategy-is the true edge.

Chapter 11

The Exit is Always Someone Else – Unless You Let It Be You

A New Framework for Trading Without Becoming Someone Else's Exit

If you've followed the journey through this book so far, one thing should be clear:

Most traders don't lose because they make one bad decision. They lose because their **entire framework is flawed.** They trade from a place of reaction, not preparation. From emotion, not structure. From urgency, not awareness.

The truth is: someone is always the exit. Someone is always the last to buy, the last to believe, the last to hold.

To avoid being that person, you need a new framework. One that:

- Prioritises **context over confirmation.**

- Demands **confluence, not convenience.**

- Uses **price action as a language**, not just lines and patterns.

This framework doesn't rely on predictions. It focuses on positioning-mentally and structurally-so you're never the liquidity someone else uses to get out.

This new framework begins with a **change in lens:**

- From *looking for trades* to *waiting for traps to spring-and avoiding them*.

- From *chasing confirmation* to *analysing context*.

- From *rushing into breakout moves* to *positioning before the herd notices*.

Ask before every trade:

- Who is likely buying here?

- Am I early enough to matter-or late enough to be used?

- Is this clarity-or am I seeking comfort?

If you can't answer these without doubt, you're entering the market **as someone else's exit, not on your own terms**.

Trading is not about control over outcomes. It's about control over **where in the cycle you participate**.

Thinking Like a Strategist, Not a Participant

Most retail traders think like participants. They wait for action. They react to price. They respond to noise. They are always **inside** the market-emotionally, mentally, financially.

Smart money thinks like strategists.

They observe from the outside first.

They ask:

- Where is the crowd going to act-and how can I use that?

- What information is being distributed-and why now?

- How does the structure serve the informed, not the reactive?

They think in terms of **probability, positioning, and pressure points**-not charts and candles.

The strategist sees the market not as an invitation-but as a **puzzle**.

Before entering, they map:

- **What the market wants retail to believe**, and

- **What institutions are likely doing behind the scenes.**

Participants chase price.

Strategists stalk opportunity.

A strategist knows that sometimes **the best trade is no trade**. That missing the move is better than forcing one. That waiting for others to step into traps **creates clarity for a clean entry**.

If you trade to be right, you're a participant.

If you trade to exploit asymmetric risk with preparation, you're thinking like a strategist.

Redefining How You Enter, Hold, and Exit

The traditional retail trading cycle is broken.

- **Entry**: Triggered by excitement, headlines, or chart patterns without context.

- **Hold**: Defined by hope and hesitation.

- **Exit**: Driven by fear, regret, or desperation.

To avoid being the exit, you must **redefine each phase** of your trade.

Entry

- Must be based on confluence of factors: price, volume, sentiment, time.

- Should only occur when the trade idea aligns with a broader narrative.

Hold

- Needs structure: key levels, conditions, and partial exit plans.

- Emotion must be removed through predefined milestones.

Exit

- Should never be improvised.

- Should occur at predetermined zones-or if conditions for the trade idea dissolve.

Smart money doesn't "see how it goes."

They know where they're going before they start.

A refined framework asks:

- What **must happen** to justify staying in the trade?

- At what point is the **original thesis no longer valid**?

- Where will smart money likely exit-and am I aligned with or against that move?

Retail holds out of **emotional commitment**. Informed traders hold because the **trade idea is still intact**.

Redefining exit also includes **accepting small losses early**-because a controlled exit is always better than being forced to exit on someone else's terms.

You didn't fail if you exited early.

You failed only if you exited **after the trap snapped shut around you**.

From Victim to Predator: Adopting the Smart Money Mindset

To stop being the exit, you must stop trading like prey.

This doesn't mean becoming manipulative or aggressive. It means adopting the mindset of a predator-not emotionally, but structurally.

The smart money mindset is:

- Calm in silence.

- Focused in chaos.

- Patient with preparation.

- Ruthless in execution.

It understands that **liquidity is created by emotion, and emotion is predictable.**

Retail is the victim when it:

- Chases price.

- Ignores volume.

- Trusts headlines.

- Reacts to noise.

The predator watches, waits, and then strikes **where emotion is loudest and structure is weakest.**

Becoming the predator doesn't mean you must exploit others. It means you must **remove yourself from the cycle of being exploited.**

That means:

- Using retail psychology as a **risk filter**, not a trade trigger.

- Waiting for **extremes**-of sentiment, structure, or setup.

- Never acting unless **reward outweighs risk** and **the herd is showing its hand.**

The predator mindset is not about more trades. It's about:

- **Better timing,**

- **Clearer intent**, and

- **Precise alignment with institutional behaviour.**

You won't win every time.

But you will stop losing for the wrong reasons

.And that's what keeps you from ever being the exit again.

Conclusion and Key Takeaways

You've seen how the game is played. You've understood the mechanics, the traps, the psychology, and the patterns. But this final section was about something far more powerful: **how not to be used**.

This was your shift from student to strategist. From retail follower to informed operator. From being someone else's exit to becoming your own edge.

In this section, you've learned how to **reverse the role**-from the one reacting to the one observing (Chapter 8). You've understood that being contrarian is not about defiance, but about **confirmation and control** (Chapter 9). You've seen that the market doesn't beat you with complexity-it beats you with emotion-and you now have the tools to manage yours (Chapter 10). And finally, you've redefined your entire framework for entering, holding, and exiting trades-not as a participant, but as a **strategist with discipline, clarity, and edge** (Chapter 11).

The game doesn't change.

But your role in it has.

Key Takeaways

- **You are no longer the exit.** That identity was built on emotion, urgency, and lack of awareness. You now operate from structure, patience, and clarity.

- **Distribution leaves clues.** Failed rallies, volume anomalies, sentiment extremes-they are not noise. They are footprints of smart money. And now you know how to see them.

- **Contrarian thinking is useless without confirmation.** It's not about being early. It's about being *late and right*-with structure, sentiment, and evidence on your side.

- **Discipline is not willpower-it's design.** Tools like journaling, structured reflection, and reset routines protect you from the real enemy: *your own impulses*.

- **The market is not your adversary-it is your mirror.** It reflects who you are under pressure. When you change, your outcomes change-not because the market softened, but because you hardened.

- **Being a predator is not about manipulation-it's about precision.** You now enter with intent. You exit with clarity. And you wait with patience that most can't match.

This is not the end. This is where your real edge begins. Because knowledge without behaviour is noise.

But knowledge with discipline-that's conviction. That's power. That's how you never become **the exit** again.

Final Note – The Reader's Manifesto

Don't Be the Exit – Escape the Retail Trap, Outsmarting the Big Players

This book was not written to teach you how to predict markets.
It was written to help you **understand what you're participating in.**

Because once you see the invisible game-the traps, the cycles, the engineered narratives-you can no longer unsee it. You begin to trade differently. You begin to think differently. You stop asking, *"Is this the right stock?"* and start asking, *"Whose story am I buying?"*

Let this be your new lens:

- Not chasing momentum.

- Not reacting to noise.

- Not needing permission to enter-or validation to exit.

- You are no longer the liquidity.

- You are no longer the last one in.

- You are no longer the reason someone else got to exit at a premium.

- You are not retail.

- You are **informed capital**.

- You move with intent. You execute with silence. You wait like a sniper.

- You enter on clarity. You exit on your own terms.

- You do not trade for dopamine.

- You do not seek applause.

- You do not fear missing out-because you know that real trades come not from noise, but from structure.

- You do not become the exit-because you've learned to build your own.

Your Manifesto Starts Here:

- I do not chase price. I chase conviction.

- I do not react to headlines. I read the tape.

- I do not seek crowd validation. I seek context.

- I do not fear being late. I fear being wrong.

- I do not trade to be busy. I trade to be effective.

- I do not become the exit. I create the exit.

Let the crowd follow. Let the noise grow.

You are no longer part of it. You are **beyond it**.

The game is still rigged. The traps are still active.

But now, so are you-

Awake. Equipped. Unshakeable.

- You are not retail anymore.
- You are not the exit anymore.
- You are the informed minority.
- And from this moment on,
- you will trade like it.

103

APPENDICES & EXTRAS

IPO Red Flag Checklist – Spotting Dilution Traps

In the world of public markets, **IPOs (Initial Public Offerings)** are often marketed as exclusive invitations to "get in early." They are wrapped in optimism, framed as growth stories, and paraded with high-profile narratives. But for the seasoned trader or the informed investor, the first question is not *what is being sold*-it is *why now, and by whom?*

When retail traders chase IPOs without context, they risk stepping into **a structured liquidity event**, designed not to offer opportunity-but to enable **early investors to exit.**

The following checklist is not merely technical. It is designed to **arm you with a thinking framework**-to assess, not just react; to question, not just assume.

1. High Insider Selling Through Offer for Sale (OFS) Components

What to look for:

A large proportion of the IPO consists of **Offer for Sale** rather than **Fresh Issue.**

Why it matters:

If the majority of the proceeds are not going to the company, but to existing shareholders cashing out, it's a clear signal:

This IPO isn't for capital expansion. It's for **liquidity exit.**

Especially beware when:

- Founders, PE funds, or VCs are offloading aggressively.

- There's no compelling use of proceeds aligned with long-term growth.

2. Aggressive Valuation Without Profit Visibility

What to look for:

Valuation multiples (Price-to-Sales, EV/EBITDA) are significantly higher than peers, particularly in a loss-making or low-margin business.

Why it matters:

Narratives are being priced in-not results. These IPOs rely on forward stories that may never materialise. If future growth is already priced in today, the only way is down unless reality exceeds euphoria.

Valuation gaps = expectation traps.

Ask: Would I buy this business privately at this price? If not, why accept it publicly?

3. Recency Bias in Financials or Performance Spikes Pre-IPO

What to look for:

Unusual growth, profitability, or margin improvement in the 12–18 months leading to the IPO.

Why it matters:

Window-dressing is real. Companies often **boost numbers** before listing-via one-off contracts, expense deferrals, or temporary accounting tactics.

If the trajectory seems "too good, too sudden," it often is.

4. Lack of Lock-In for Significant Shareholders

What to look for:

Insiders are either exempt from long lock-in periods, or have **loopholes allowing early exit** post-listing.

Why it matters:

The absence of meaningful "skin in the game" is a red flag. If those closest to the business aren't required-or willing-to stay invested, what incentive do they have to create long-term value?

If insiders can sell but you can't, **you are not a partner-you're the exit.**

5. Use of Proceeds Lacking Clarity or Strategic Depth

What to look for:

Vague statements in the DRHP (Draft Red Herring Prospectus) like:

- "To meet general corporate purposes."

- "To repay existing debt" (without clarity on impact or sustainability).

- "For future growth" with no operational roadmap.

Why it matters:

If the capital raised isn't going into tangible, measurable growth projects, then the listing serves no strategic purpose. It's a financial event, not a business one.

Smart IPOs clarify:

- Where funds will go.

- What outcomes are expected.

- How this will benefit shareholders long-term.

6. Sectoral Euphoria and Timing Correlation

What to look for:

The IPO rides a hot theme-EV, fintech, AI, platform businesses-during a time of extreme sentiment or market rally.

Why it matters:

Strong sectors attract weak businesses. When market demand is high, even unprofitable or structurally weak companies **rush to list**, exploiting appetite over substance.

A legitimate business may still list under these conditions, but **context matters**. If too many IPOs crowd the same space in a short window, someone is exiting-**and it's not the early investors.**

7. Management History and Governance Track Record

What to look for:

- Prior businesses run by the same founders.

- Past regulatory issues.

- Corporate governance transparency (board independence, audit trail, disclosures).

Why it matters:

Trust is not built during roadshows-it is earned over time. If management lacks a credible history, or if transparency is compromised, listing status will not fix what's broken internally.

Governance red flags lead to **post-listing breakdowns**-and by then, retail is already trapped.

8. Grey Market Premium (GMP) Hype Without Anchor Strength

What to look for:

High GMP in the unofficial market, driven by buzz-not by strong institutional anchor participation.

Why it matters:

GMP hype is seductive-but unreliable. Retail often uses GMP to judge listing success, but **smart money uses it to exit into retail exuberance.**

If GMP soars but:

- Anchor investors are few,

- Or allocation to them is weak,

- Or they exit early post-listing...

...it's a **pop-and-drop** setup in disguise.

9. Poor Post-Listing Float Management

What to look for:

Once listed:

- Stock sees weak or no follow-through.

- Volumes surge but price struggles.

- Key early backers start trimming stake aggressively.

Why it matters:

Distribution has begun. Retail, driven by FOMO or belief in the brand, enters when risk is highest. The trap was not in the listing-it was in the **post-listing liquidity window.**

Strong IPOs consolidate with support. Weak ones start fading the moment cameras turn off.

10. Overuse of Buzzwords Without Business Depth

What to look for:

DRHPs or marketing materials flooded with language like:

- "Disruptive innovation"

- "AI-enabled ecosystem"

- "Next-gen platform play"

Why it matters:

Narratives are used to inflate perception. If the business can't explain **how** it generates revenue, builds moats, or turns a profit-but spends paragraphs telling you it's a unicorn-it's time to step back.

Simplicity is often a sign of truth.

Complexity cloaks dilution.

Final Thought

IPO participation isn't about being early-it's about being **informed**. When insiders exit, they do so with planning, context, and structure. Retail traders must learn to **read the narrative, not just react to it**.

This checklist is not a reason to avoid all IPOs. It is a reason to approach them **with eyes open and emotion shut**. Because every IPO creates liquidity. The only question is-**will it come from you, or will it be given to you?**

Retail vs Smart Money

Side-by-side Behavioural Analysis

Understanding the behavioural gap between retail traders and smart money is not about labelling one group as unintelligent or inexperienced. It is about recognising the differences in mindset, execution, risk perception, and timing-so that the informed trader can consciously cross the chasm between reacting to markets and thinking ahead of them.

The following table is not just a comparison of habits. It is a mirror-one that reflects where most traders go wrong, and how those who win approach the same market differently.

Each contrast below is drawn from recurring, observable patterns that repeat across cycles, asset classes, and trader profiles.

Category	Retail Trader Behaviour	Smart Money Behaviour
Mindset	Emotional, reactive, seeks excitement	Strategic, detached, seeks edge
Trade Trigger	Based on price movement, news, or social media hype	Based on structure, volume, sentiment imbalance
Timing	Enters late, exits late	Enters early, exits into strength
Information Source	Relies on headlines, forums, influencer opinions	Relies on internal data, market structure, sentiment signals
Entry Criteria	Confirmation through breakout or news	Anticipation through accumulation zones and crowd behavior
Exit Logic	Exits in panic or greed	Exits at pre-defined levels, often during peak euphoria
Risk Perception	Focuses on potential reward; underestimates risk	Assesses downside first; reward is secondary to protection
Position Sizing	Based on emotion, often inconsistent	Based on volatility, conviction, and capital preservation rules
Reaction to Volatility	Overreacts, misreads noise as signal	Uses volatility as opportunity to trap or accumulate
Trade Frequency	High—feels the need to be constantly active	Low—waits for high-quality, asymmetric opportunities
Use of Indicators	Uses many; seeks signal validation	Uses few; focuses on price action, volume, liquidity
Behaviour Around Tops	Buys euphorically; trusts media and breakouts	Sells quietly; sees euphoria as a cue to exit
Behaviour Around Bottoms	Panics or freezes; avoids at value zones	Accumulates patiently as others exit in fear
Accountability	Blames market, manipulation, bad luck	Tracks process, reviews decisions, adapts systems
Learning Loop	Repeats mistakes emotionally	Refines thesis logically through journaling and review
Market Identity	Sees the market as adversarial, unfair	Accepts the market as neutral, but manipulatable
Execution Philosophy	Acts based on feelings or recent trades	Acts based on preparation, probability, and context
Psychological Anchor	Trades to feel right, avoid regret, chase hope	Trades to express an edge, limit exposure, stay disciplined

How to Use This Table

This isn't meant to shame retail habits-it's meant to illuminate the path forward. Every trader starts on the left-hand side of this table. The journey to the right side is not mechanical-it is mental.

Ask yourself:

- Which side do my habits reflect in times of uncertainty?
- Which 3 retail behaviours have cost me the most?
- Which smart money behaviours am I ready to commit to?

The moment you start trading like smart money is not when your P&L changes. It's when your decisions become boring, methodical, and rational-while others chase, panic, and hope.

Final Insight

Smart money isn't always right. But they lose less when they're wrong, and they win bigger when they're right-because they enter earlier, exit better, and execute without emotional friction.

Your edge begins when you stop asking, "What's the market doing?" And start asking, "Who's participating-and what are they feeling?"

Because trading is never just about charts. It's about who you are when the market starts moving against you.

Real-world Events Where Retail Was the Exit

Retail traders often act last—entering when confidence is highest, narratives are loudest, and risk is least visible. In contrast, institutional players enter during uncertainty and exit into euphoria. The following examples illustrate this psychological pattern in action.

Each case is a **real-world example**—legally safe, fact-based, and selected for the valuable lessons it offers about **timing, sentiment, and exit liquidity**.

INDIA

1. Paytm IPO (2021)

Event: India's largest-ever IPO at the time, Paytm debuted at a valuation exceeding ₹1.4 lakh crore.

Retail Action: Enthusiastically subscribed by retail investors amid tech optimism.

Smart Money Action: Early investors, including venture capitalists and promoters, offloaded significant stakes.

Outcome: The stock fell over 27% on listing day and continued to decline, eroding massive value for retail entrants.

Insight: High-profile IPOs can be **exit windows**, not entry points, when optimism is priced in.

2. Yes Bank Collapse (2018–2020)

Event: Once a darling of Indian banking, Yes Bank faced a liquidity and governance crisis.

Retail Action: Bought heavily on dips, driven by belief in a turnaround and low price.

Smart Money Action: Institutions exited or wrote down exposure during early stages of trouble.

Outcome: The stock plummeted over 90%, and a reconstruction scheme followed.

Insight: Falling prices don't always mean value— they often mean institutional exits have already begun.

3. Zomato Post-IPO Sell-Off (2021–2022)

Event: Zomato's IPO saw stellar listing gains and massive retail interest.

Retail Action: Continued buying even after a parabolic post-listing move.

Smart Money Action: Pre-IPO investors, including Info Edge, trimmed their stakes during rallies.

Outcome: Stock corrected more than 50% from highs, leaving retail caught at inflated levels.

Insight: Post-listing rallies are often **distribution zones**—not long-term value zones.

4. Reliance Power IPO (2008)

Event: Hugely anticipated IPO during India's infrastructure boom.

Retail Action: Subscribed enthusiastically; oversubscription reached record levels.

Smart Money Action: Promoters and early backers sold into demand.

Outcome: Listed at a premium, then crashed; investors suffered heavy losses for years.

Insight: Narrative-driven IPOs can mark the **end of a cycle**, not its beginning.

5. Suzlon Energy Boom and Bust (2007–2009)

Event: Suzlon became a popular renewable energy bet in mid-2000s.

Retail Action: Rushed in during price momentum and media coverage.

Smart Money Action: Exited during aggressive price rallies.

Outcome: Declined over 95% over subsequent years due to debt and order issues.

Insight: Early hype in emerging sectors is often a **smart money exit window.**

6. Adani Group Stocks (2022–2023)

Event: Rapid multibagger rallies followed by sharp drawdowns after short-seller reports.

Retail Action: Bought aggressively at elevated valuations, driven by momentum and retail-led narratives.

Smart Money Action: Institutions gradually reduced exposure or hedged risks ahead of volatility.

Outcome: Sharp corrections led to significant erosion in paper gains.

Insight: When **momentum becomes blind belief**, smart money prepares to exit.

UNITED STATES

7. GameStop Short Squeeze (2021)

Event: A historic retail-driven rally initiated on Reddit's r/WallStreetBets.

Retail Action: Bought heavily during peak volatility, driven by collective euphoria.

Smart Money Action: Institutions who entered early exited into the price spike; others hedged positions or shorted again post-rally.

Outcome: Price collapsed from ~$480 to under $50 within weeks.

Insight: Retail-led rallies without fundamentals often become **exit ramps for pros**.

8. Robinhood IPO (2021)

Event: Robinhood's IPO was marketed as a "democratised listing" with shares allotted to app users.

Retail Action: Bought based on brand loyalty and excitement over participation.

Smart Money Action: VC firms and early stakeholders used the event to liquidate at high valuations.

Outcome: Stock declined over 70% from its peak within the first year.

Insight: When **access feels easy**, value may already be extracted.

9. Coinbase IPO (2021)

Event: The largest direct listing of a crypto platform amid peak crypto mania.

Retail Action: Entered at ~$328–$400 levels, driven by Bitcoin's surge.

Smart Money Action: Early investors and insiders sold nearly $5 billion worth of stock at listing.

Outcome: Stock corrected sharply as Bitcoin cooled off.

Insight: High-profile listings often **coincide with cycle tops**.

10. WeWork Failed IPO (2019)

Event: Heavily hyped IPO collapsed after governance and valuation scrutiny.

Retail Action: Would have likely entered had the IPO gone live.

Smart Money Action: Attempted to offload inflated valuation onto public market.

Outcome: IPO was withdrawn; valuation collapsed from $47B to sub-$10B.

Insight: Not all traps trigger. **Due diligence sometimes stops the bleeding.**

11. Nikola Motors Pump and Dump (2020)

Event: EV hype led to Nikola's stock skyrocketing despite lack of revenue or products.

Retail Action: Bought aggressively on social media hype and comparisons to Tesla.

Smart Money Action: Insiders and backers sold during price surge.

Outcome: Stock dropped over 90% as fraud allegations surfaced.

Insight: Retail emotion + narrative = perfect exit conditions for insiders.

12. Beyond Meat IPO Surge and Fade (2019)

Event: Beyond Meat's stock surged 160% on listing day and climbed 800%+ in two months.

Retail Action: Entered late in the rally, fuelled by FOMO.

Smart Money Action: Insiders sold shares post-lock-in expiration.

Outcome: Stock fell sharply from highs, retracing over 70%.

Insight: Parabolic price action in new sectors = high-probability smart money exit zones.

Glossary of Key Terms

A

Accumulation

A phase where institutional players gradually build positions, usually during periods of low volatility and minimal attention. Often precedes a breakout or uptrend.

Anchor Investor

A large institutional investor who commits to a major IPO or offer, often providing credibility and perceived confidence in the issue.

B

Bear Trap

A false breakdown that lures traders into short positions before reversing higher—triggered to create liquidity and force covering.

Breakout

A move where price crosses a key support or resistance level. Breakouts can be real (with volume and follow-through) or engineered (to trap liquidity).

C

Capitulation

A point of emotional surrender in a falling market where retail traders panic and sell, often marking a market bottom.

Confirmation Bias

The tendency to seek out information that supports an existing belief or position, while ignoring contradictory data.

Confluence

The alignment of multiple technical or contextual signals (e.g., support zone + volume + sentiment), adding conviction to a trade setup.

Crowd Confirmation

A psychological trigger where traders feel safe because everyone seems to be on the same side. It often occurs near tops, when risk is highest and the majority is fully positioned.

Chasing the Exit

A condition where retail participants attempt to exit trades en masse after smart money has already left, usually during sharp drawdowns or panic selling.

D

Distribution

The process where smart money exits positions into rising prices and crowd enthusiasm—opposite of accumulation.

Dow Theory – Markup Phase

Stage 2 in the Dow Theory cycle where price trends upward. It's where institutions begin offloading positions into strength.

E

Exit Liquidity

Retail traders who buy at the top of a move, unknowingly providing the liquidity that allows institutions or insiders to exit their positions.

Euphoria Candle

A large bullish candle often fuelled by emotional buying and news hype—commonly used by smart money to distribute into.

Engineered Exit

A price move, breakout, or news event used by institutions to draw in retail volume and create the liquidity needed to offload positions strategically.

Exit Trap

A setup where price appears to offer a clean exit (e.g., small bounce after a drop), only to reverse sharply. Retail exits emotionally; smart money buys the liquidity.

F

False Breakout

A move above a resistance (or below support) that quickly reverses, trapping breakout traders and often leading to sharp counter moves.

FOMO (Fear of Missing Out)

A psychological driver causing traders to enter late into a trend due to social pressure or rising prices.

Front-Run

A tactic where traders or institutions anticipate crowd behaviour or news and position ahead of it—often leading to outsized gains or better exits.

Flush Candle

A large red candle, usually on panic volume, where weak hands are shaken out. These often serve as smart money entry zones, while retail exits in fear.

G

Gamification

Design techniques used by brokers or platforms to make trading feel like a game—rewarding frequency over quality, encouraging compulsive trading.

H

Herd Mentality

The tendency of retail traders to follow crowd consensus, especially in euphoric or fearful markets—often leading to poor timing.

Hope Exit

An emotionally driven exit strategy where a trader holds onto a losing position too long, hoping for a turnaround, then exits at the worst possible time.

I

Iceberg Order

A large institutional order split into smaller visible orders to hide real size and avoid triggering volatility or alerting other participants.

Institutional Footprint

Subtle signs in price, volume, or behaviour that suggest accumulation, distribution, or large-player activity.

J

J-Curve Trap

A setup where initial losses are rationalised as short-term drawdowns, often leading to longer-term capital erosion if not exited early.

L

Liquidity Event

A moment, such as an IPO or news breakout, that creates the volume needed for large investors to exit positions without disrupting price too early.

Lock-In Period

The time during which insiders are restricted from selling shares post-IPO. The end of this period often signals potential supply pressure.

Late Entry Syndrome

A behavioural pattern where retail traders consistently enter trends after they've matured—typically due to FOMO, media hype, or peer pressure.

M

Market Depth

The ability of a market to absorb large orders without impacting price. Illiquid stocks are more prone to manipulation and slippage.

Markup Phase

See: Dow Theory – Markup Phase

Media Pump

The strategic use of news, upgrades, or influencer narratives to create buying interest—often into a smart money distribution phase.

Mass Retail Participation Zone

A price area where retail enters in large numbers due to perceived confirmation. Often coincides with smart money distribution levels.

Mental Liquidity Event

A psychological tipping point where retail traders become sellers not because of strategy, but because of fear, regret, or collective emotional panic.

N

Narrative Trading

Trading based on a compelling story or theme (e.g., AI, green energy), often regardless of underlying fundamentals or valuations.

O

OFS (Offer for Sale)

A component of an IPO or secondary offering where existing shareholders sell their holdings to the public—often used as an exit mechanism by early investors.

P

Psychological Stop

A mental threshold beyond which a trader can no longer tolerate loss—often leads to reactive exits or revenge trades if not planned.

Predator Zone

A setup or phase where smart money anticipates retail emotion (greed or panic) and uses it to execute highly asymmetric trades.

Participation Fallacy

The belief that being "in the move" is more important than the quality of the move, leading to poor entries and becoming someone else's exit.

R

Retail Exhaustion

A point where most retail participants are already committed to a trend, leaving no more buyers and increasing risk of reversal.

Risk Asymmetry

A setup where potential upside far outweighs downside. Smart money seeks these conditions before committing capital.

Retail Trap

Any engineered or coincidental setup that lures retail participants to act emotionally—whether through fake breakouts, IPOs, or euphoric headlines.

S

Smart Money

Large, strategic market participants (institutions, funds, insiders) with superior resources, information access, and patience.

Stop Hunt

A sharp move designed to trigger stop-loss orders before reversing in the original direction. Often used to shake out weak hands.

Structure

The contextual makeup of price movement—ranges, trends, retests—that informs where real opportunity or risk lies.

Sniper Entry

A highly selective, high-conviction entry taken only when multiple conditions (structure, sentiment, volume) align. Emphasises quality over quantity.

Structured Exit

An exit plan defined before entering the trade. Helps avoid emotional decision-making and ensures the trader doesn't become someone else's liquidity.

T

Technical Trap

A price movement that mimics a valid technical breakout or breakdown but is engineered to trap and reverse on retail participants.

Trailing Exit

A method of exiting by moving stop-loss levels upward as price advances—often used to lock in profits during momentum phases.

Trap Volume

Volume that appears during euphoric or panicked moves, largely made up of emotional retail participants. Institutions often use this to fade or absorb moves.

Transfer of Risk

The process by which smart money shifts risk onto uninformed traders—usually during euphoric rallies or news-driven spikes.

V

Volume Spike

A sudden burst in traded volume—can signal institutional activity if paired with price absorption or rejection at key levels.

Volatility Squeeze

A period of price compression that often precedes a major breakout or breakdown, used by professionals to prepare positioning.

W

Whipsaw

A sharp, erratic price movement that triggers entries or exits in both directions, often used to shake out weak hands.